Teen Resiliency-Building Workbook

Reproducible Self-Assessments, Exercises & Educational Handouts

Ester R. A. Leutenberg

John J. Liptak, EdD

Illustrated by
Amy L. Brodsky, LISW-S

whole person
Stress & Wellness Publishers
Duluth, Minnesota

Whole Person
210 West Michigan Street
Duluth, MN 55802-1908

800-247-6789

books@wholeperson.com
www.wholeperson.com

Teen Resiliency-Building Workbook
Reproducible Self-Assessments, Exercises & Educational Handouts

Copyright ©2012 by Ester R. A. Leutenberg and John J. Liptak.
All rights reserved. Except for short excerpts for review purposes
and materials in the assessment, journaling activities, and
educational handouts sections, no part of this book may be
reproduced or transmitted in any form by any means, electronic
or mechanical, including photocopying without permission in
writing from the publisher.

All efforts have been made to ensure accuracy of the information
contained in this book as of the date published. The author(s)
and the publisher expressly disclaim responsibility for any
adverse effects arising from the use or application of the
information contained herein.

Printed in the United States of America

10 9 8 7 6 5 4 3 2 1

Editorial Director: Carlene Sippola
Art Director: Joy Morgan Dey

Library of Congress Control Number: 2010936856
ISBN: 978-1-57025-263-1

Teen Resiliency

As they develop and mature, teens experience a great deal of stress in their lives. For teens, the stress they experience can be from physical changes to psychological, social and emotional stressors, and these changes can cause depression, confusion, low self-esteem, a lack of self-identity and a sense of uncertainty. Some of this stress can come from these situations . . .

- Arguments and fights at home

- Divorce of parents, caregivers, or other family members

- Pressure to get better grades

- Need to be more independent

- Wish to be better at sports, music, drama, etc.

- Pressure from peers to smoke, drink, etc.

- Victim / Target of bullying

- Career choice decisions

- Education choices decisions

- Body change

- Make friendships and community relationships

- Incentive to prove maturity

- Pressure to earn money

- Will to gain respect of teachers and other adults in the school and community

- Challenges to keep up with peers

- Pressure to do things against better judgment

Many teens face challenges stemming from stress they experience at home, school, volunteer or work settings, and with their friends. The good news is that teens who develop resilience can avoid feeling overwhelmed with the amount of stress they experience. They are able to bounce back and be strong, efficient managers of their stress and live more effective lives.

They accomplish this through building resiliency into their lives. Resiliency is a person's ability to cope with stress and hardship, bounce back to a normal state of functioning, and promote overall well-being.

(Continued)

Facts about Resiliency

Building resiliency is critical in the life of teens. It is currently called a host of other names including hardiness, psychological resilience, emotional resourcefulness, and mental resiliency. Regardless of the name you choose, resiliency is the ability of a teen to interact with the environment, handle stresses that occur, and bounce back from these stressful events. It is the process by which well-being is promoted and protection factors are activated against overwhelming feelings of stress. Teens who have developed resiliency are able to bounce back from the negative impact of difficulties.

Resiliency can be thought of as a skill that allows teens to …

- manage life's challenges, stresses, changes, and pressures effectively.
- cope with and adapt successfully to adversity.
- bounce back to a balanced state after facing a major disruption in life or career planning.

Teens have an innate ability to demonstrate resiliency as they build resiliency skills into their lives. Resilient people are able to adapt successfully under adverse circumstances such as poverty, mental illness, disasters, terrorism, physical or psychological trauma, parents' divorce, parent's job loss and financial problems, family members in prison, loss of a loved one, peer pressure, physical or sexual abuse, self-induced pressure to achieve in school, or a lack of safety. Resiliency, or a positive behavioral adaptation, is critical when people encounter any type of trauma.

Research shows that resiliency offers protection from distress and illness in the face of change or adversity. The presence of high levels of resiliency is associated with these factors: high level of happiness, self-esteem, sense of energy and vitality, optimism, self-reported health, sense of meaning and direction, and a low level of depression.

Teens who are resilient …

- work hard at school work and study because they enjoy it and want to achieve
- react in optimistic ways
- see problems and difficult situations as challenges
- take positive risks and actions
- think of changes as natural
- go with the flow
- have a high self-esteem, self-confidence, self-concept and sense of self
- thrive under challenging situations
- believe that they can influence events and their reactions to events
- recognize that with good stress comes growth
- have hope for their future
- overcome obstacles with confidence
- create goals and work at accomplishing them
- possess a keen sense of control over their life
- bounce-back from disappointments

Research also indicates that resiliency can be built through skill development by enhancing communication, developing an optimistic outlook, building a greater sense of control, creating a more realistic sense of self, and learning how to effectively deal with change. The purpose of this workbook is to provide teens with the requisite skills they need to manage their emotions and to develop and maintain resiliency.

(Continued)

Using This Book

The *Teen Resiliency-Building Workbook* contains five separate sections to help participants learn more about themselves and how to build the resiliency which will enable them to thrive in times of adversity, change and stress. They will learn about the importance of building resiliency skills to turn change and stress into opportunities and challenges, to live life zestfully, and to take positive actions in order to live their lives with less stress.

Sections of this Book

1) OPTIMISTIC OUTLOOK SCALE helps teens identify how optimistically they view and live life.

2) SENSE OF CONTROL SCALE helps teens explore the extent to which they believe they have control over what happens in their lives.

3) SENSE-OF-SELF SCALE helps teens explore the strength of their self-esteem, self-confidence and self-concept.

4) ABILITY TO BOUNCE BACK SCALE helps teens increase their ability to bounce back and recover from a setback.

5) TYPES OF CHANGE SCALE helps teens to become aware of how well they deal with change, and to develop skills necessary to accept change.

These sections serve as avenues for individual self-reflection and participation in group experiences revolving around identified topics of importance. Each assessment includes directions for easy administration, scoring and interpretation. Each section includes exploratory activities, reflective journaling activities and educational handouts to help participants discover their own levels of resiliency. Reflective exercises and instruction also help participants to build personal and professional resiliency.

By combining reflective assessment and journaling, participants will be exposed to a powerful method of combining verbalizing and writing to reflect on and to solve problems. Participants will become more aware of the strength and weaknesses of their resiliency and find ways to build and enhance their hardiness.

Preparation for using the assessments and activities in this book is important. The authors suggest that prior to administering any of the assessments in this book, you complete them yourself. This will familiarize you with the format of the assessments, the scoring directions, the interpretation guides and the journaling activities. Although the assessments are designed to be self-administered, scored and interpreted, this familiarity will help facilitators prepare to answer questions about the assessments.

Use Codes for Confidentiality

Confidentiality is a term for any action that preserves the privacy of other people. Because teens completing the activities in this workbook might be asked to answer assessment items and to journal about and explore their relationships, the group will need to discuss confidentiality before you begin using the materials in this workbook. Maintaining confidentiality is important because it shows respect for others and allows participants to explore their feelings without hurting anyone's feelings or fearing gossip, harm or retribution.

In order to maintain confidentiality, explain to the participants that they need to assign a name code for each person or each group of people they write about as they complete the various activities in the workbook. For example, a friend named Joey who enjoys going to hockey games might be titled JLHG (Joey Loves Hockey Games) for a particular exercise. In order to protect their friends' identities, they should not use people's or groups' actual names or initials, just name codes.

The Assessments, Journaling Activities, and Educational Handouts

The Assessments, Journaling Activities, and Educational Handouts in the *Teen Resiliency-Building Workbook* are reproducible and ready to be photocopied for participants' use. Assessments contained in this book focus on self-reported data and are similar to those used by psychologists, counselors, therapists and marriage and family therapists. Accuracy and usefulness of the information provided is dependent on the truthful information that each participant provides through self-examination. By being honest, teens help themselves to learn more about how they respond and react to stress, change, and adversity in their lives, and to uncover information that might be keeping them from being as happy and/or as successful as they might be.

An assessment instrument can provide participants with valuable information about themselves; however, it cannot measure or identify everything about them. The purpose of the assessments is not to pigeon-hole certain characteristics, but rather to allow participants to explore all of their characteristics. This book contains self-assessments, not tests. Tests measure knowledge or whether something is right or wrong. For the assessments in this book, there are no right or wrong answers. These assessments ask for personal opinions or attitudes about a topic of importance in the participant's career and life.

When administering assessments in this workbook, remember that the items are generically written so that they will be applicable to a wide variety of people. They will not account for every possible variable for every person. The assessments are not specifically tailored to one person. Use them to help participants identify possible negative themes in their lives and to find ways to break the hold that these patterns and their effects have.

Advise teen participants taking the assessments they should not spend too much time trying to analyze the content of the questions; their initial response to each item will most likely be true. Regardless of individual scores, encourage participants to write and talk about their findings and their feelings pertaining to what they have discovered about themselves. Resilient teens are able to adapt successfully and cope with stress and catastrophe. They have the ability to bounce back to a balanced state after disruption or transition. Exploring resiliency-building exercises will be helpful to the teens now and as they mature into adulthood.

A particular score on any assessment does not guarantee a participant's level of happiness. Use discretion when using any of the information or feedback provided in this workbook. The use of these assessments should not be substituted for consultation and/or counseling from a psychological or medical professional.

Thanks to the following professionals whose input in this book has been so valuable!
Kathy Khalsa, OTR/L
Jay Leutenberg
Kathy Liptak, Ed.D.
Eileen Regen, M.Ed., CJE

Layout of the Book

The *Teen Resiliency-Building Workbook* is designed to be used either independently or as part of an integrated curriculum. You may administer one of the assessments and the journaling exercises to an individual or a group with whom you are working, or you may administer a number of the assessments over one or more days.

This book includes the following reproducible pages in the first five sections:

- **Assessment Instruments** – Self-assessment inventories with scoring directions and interpretation materials. Group facilitators can choose one or more of the activities relevant to their participants.

- **Activity Handouts** – Practical questions and activities that prompt self-reflection and promote self-understanding. These questions and activities foster introspection and promote pro-social behaviors.

- **Quotations** – Quotations are used in each section to provide insight and promote reflection. Participants will be asked to select one or more of the quotations and journal about what the quotations mean to them.

- **Reflective Questions for Journaling** – Self-exploration activities and journaling exercises specific to each assessment to enhance self-discovery, learning, and healing.

- **Educational Handouts** – Handouts designed to enhance instruction can be used by individuals or in groups to promote a positive understanding of managing conflict. They can be distributed, scanned and converted into masters for overheads or transparencies, projected or written on boards and/or discussed.

Who Should Use This Program?

This book has been designed as a practical tool for helping professional therapists, counselors, marriage and family therapists, psychologists, teachers, group leaders, etc. Depending on the role of the professional using the *Teen Resiliency-Building Workbook* and the specific group's needs, these sections can be used individually, combined, or implemented as part of an integrated curriculum for a more comprehensive approach.

Why Use Self-Assessments?

- Self-assessments are important in teaching various anger management skills because they help participants to engage in these ways:
- Become aware of the primary motivators that guide their behavior
- Explore and learn to "let go" of troublesome habits and behavioral patterns learned in childhood
- Examine the effects of unconscious childhood messages
- Gain insight and "a wake-up call" for behavioral change
- Focus thinking on behavioral goals for change
- Uncover personal resources that can help them to cope better with problems and difficulties
- Explore personal characteristics without judgment
  Identify personal strengths and weaknesses

Because the assessments are presented in a straightforward and easy-to-use format, individuals can self-administer, score and interpret each assessment at their own pace.

Introduction for the Participant

The media sometimes portrays the teen years as easy, happy-go-lucky years in which you wear the right clothes, fit in well with all your friends, have a great home life and do well in school. As you know, life as a teen can be very different from that image. You may face problems at home, relationship issues, bullying, school situations and experience the loss of loved ones. Why are some people able to go through really rough times and bounce back, while others are unable to do so? **Resiliency!**

Resiliency is described as your ability to bounce back and cope with challenges in your life.

Resiliency is the ability to . . .

- deal effectively with stress and adversity

- successfully handle changes in life

- withstand grief and accept loss

- creatively adapt to life challenges.

Psychologically resilient teens tend to have less stress, anxiety and depression. They tend to do better in school, home, work or volunteer jobs and with friends and in the community. Remember the building-resiliency process is a personal journey that can help you develop lifelong skills to strengthen your ability to adapt to change and cope with stress.

The *Teen Resiliency-Building Workbook* is designed to help you learn more about yourself; identify the stresses and challenges in your life; explore how you have dealt with adversity in the past; develop resiliency skills and a resiliency mindset; and find better ways to use these newfound skills to deal effectively with whatever setbacks you encounter in life. You will be encouraged to complete assessments, journaling activities and exercises. Because active involvement and "doing" is as important as learning theories, it is critical that you take the time to complete all of the skill-building exercises.

Confidentiality

You will be asked to respond to assessments and exercises, and to journal about some experiences in your relationships. Everyone has the right to confidentiality, and you need to honor the right of privacy of the people you may be writing about. Think about it this way – you would not want someone writing things about you that other people could read. Your family, friends and anyone else you include in the exercises deserve this respect also.

In order to maintain the confidentiality of your friends and family members, assign code names to people or groups, based on things you know about them. For example, a friend named Sherry who loves to wear purple might be coded as SWP (Sherry Wears Purple).

Do not use any person's or group's actual name when you are listing people or groups of people – use only name codes.

Teen Building Resiliency Workbook
TABLE OF CONTENTS

TABLE OF CONTENTS

TABLE OF CONTENTS

TABLE OF CONTENTS

Section V: Types of Change Scale

Types of Change Scale

Exercises

Journaling Activities

Educational Handouts

SECTION I:
Optimistic Outlook Scale

Name_____

Date_____

Optimistic Outlook Scale Directions

Some people see the glass half full, while others see it half empty. Those who see the glass half full are optimists; those who see the glass half empty are pessimists. As an optimist, regardless of transitions, setbacks, or disappointments, the person looks at the bright side and sees the possibilities life has to offer. Optimists expect good things to happen, expect to be able to solve problems efficiently, and plan to accomplish their life and work goals. They go through life with positive outlooks and are content most of the time.

Optimists maintain a positive world-view. Pessimists think negatively and cynically about the world. The Optimistic Outlook Scale is designed to help you assess your outlook when negative and positive things happen in your life.

This scale contains 40 statements that are divided into four resiliency categories. Read each of the statements and decide whether or not the statement describes you. For each of the statements listed, circle the number of your response on the line to the right of each statement.

In the following example, the circled 4 indicates the statement is very much like the person completing the assessment:

	Very Much Like Me	Usually Like Me	Not Usually Like Me	Not Like Me
1. When things go wrong, I remain hopeful	(4)	3	2	1

This is not a test and there are no right or wrong answers. Do not spend too much time thinking about your answers. Your initial response will be the most true for you. Be sure to respond to every statement.

(Turn to the next page and begin)

Optimistic Outlook Scale

	Very Much Like Me	Usually Like Me	Not Usually Like Me	Not Like Me
1. When things go wrong, I remain hopeful 4	3	2	1
2. A lot of situations do not have a "silver lining" 1	2	3	4
3. I can always see the light at the end of the tunnel. . . . 4	3	2	1
4. I often feel hopeless. 1	2	3	4
5. I look on the bright side of things 4	3	2	1
6. I'm usually optimistic about my future 4	3	2	1
7. I am unhappy a lot of the time 1	2	3	4
8. I rarely get depressed when I think about the future. . . 4	3	2	1
9. I do not wait for happiness to find me 4	3	2	1
10. I often feel helpless when things change. 1	2	3	4

H · TOTAL = _____

	Very Much Like Me	Usually Like Me	Not Usually Like Me	Not Like Me
11. In uncertain times, I usually expect the best 4	3	2	1
12. If something can go wrong, it will. 1	2	3	4
13. I usually expect things to go my way 4	3	2	1
14. Things usually don't work out the way I want them to 1	2	3	4
15. I am afraid to hope that good things will happen to me. 1	2	3	4
16. I often say "good things never happen to me". 1	2	3	4
17. My life is filled with problems 1	2	3	4
18. Even if I have failed in the past, I do not expect to fail again. 4	3	2	
19. I usually maintain a positive attitude in life 4	3	2	1
20. I feel like I have no control over what happens in my life 1	2	3	4

L · TOTAL = _____

(Continued on the next page)

(Optimistic Outlook Scale continued)

	Very Much Like Me	Usually Like Me	Not Usually Like Me	Not Like Me
21. I usually talk about positive things	4	3	2	1
22. I often do not look for the good in people.	1	2	3	4
23. I see the "glass as half full" not "half empty"	4	3	2	1
24. I have had a hard time seeing many possibilities in a situation	1	2	3	4
25. Every day holds numerous opportunities..	4	3	2	1
26. When faced with a challenge, my first thought is "I can do this!"	4	3	2	1
27. I am able to be positive even when things do not go my way.	4	3	2	1
28. I see every day as a new opportunity at life.	4	3	2	1
29. I often find myself waiting for happiness to find me . . .	1	2	3	4
30. I believe that things will work out the way I want	4	3	2	1

A - TOTAL = _____

	Very Much Like Me	Usually Like Me	Not Usually Like Me	Not Like Me
31. I set goals and work toward them	4	3	2	1
32. I often lack confidence in myself	1	2	3	4
33. I believe I can do whatever I set my mind to	4	3	2	1
34. I am not a quitter.	4	3	2	1
35. I will take positive risks even if I fail	4	3	2	1
36. I often blame my unhappiness on others.	1	2	3	4
37. I don't let obstacles get in my way.	4	3	2	1
38. I rarely blame others when bad things happen to me	4	3	2	1
39. When people say "it's impossible," I usually believe them	1	2	3	4
40. I do not let others keep me from being happy.	4	3	2	1

O - TOTAL = _____

(Go to the Scoring Directions on the next page)

Optimistic Outlook Scale Scoring Directions

Resilient people are able to maintain a positive outlook. They are able to remain hopeful about their current situation and their future possibilities, expect good things to happen from their own efforts, and retain a positive attitude even when times are challenging. Resilient people work to overcome obstacles. For each of the four sections on the previous pages, total the scores you circled. Put that total on the line marked TOTAL at the end of each section.

Then, transfer your totals to the spaces below:

H - HOPE   TOTAL = _____

L – LIFE OUTLOOK   TOTAL = _____

A - ATTITUDE   TOTAL = _____

O - OVERCOMING OBSTACLES TOTAL = _____

Profile Interpretation

INDIVIDUAL SCALE SCORES	TOTAL SCALES SCORES	RESULT	INDICATIONS
Scores from 31 to 40	Scores from 121 to 160	High	You have developed and you use many skills and attitudes that lead to a positive outlook and a resilient personality.
Scores from 20 to 30	Scores from 80 to 120	Moderate	You have developed and you use some skills and attitudes that lead to a positive outlook and a resilient personality.
Scores from 10 to 19	Scores from 40 to 79	Low	You have not developed or used many skills and attitudes that lead to a positive outlook and a resilient personality.

Read the descriptions on the following pages and complete the exercises that are included. No matter how you scored, low, moderate or high, you will benefit from these exercises.

Hope

Hope can be described as a mindset consisting of a positive view of the future for yourself and others. Remaining hopeful over the course of your life is at the core of resiliency and the ability to bounce back while facing problems and the stress that goes along with those problems. Having hope will guide you with resiliency while you achieve your goals and dreams.

Respond to the following questions to identify your hope patterns:

What does this quote by Emily Dickinson mean to you?

"Hope is the thing with feathers."

_____

_____

_____

_____

What happened in your life that caused you to stop hoping?

_____

_____

_____

_____

Where do you believe your sources of hope, or lack of hope, come from?

_____

_____

_____

_____

How has your environment affected the amount of hope you currently have?

_____

_____

_____

_____

(Continued on the next page)

Hope *(Continued)*

Where do you look for hope in your life?

_____

_____

_____

_____

What are three things you hope for?

1. _____

_____

2. _____

_____

3. _____

_____

How have your hopes changed as you have grown up?

_____

_____

_____

_____

How has hope, or a lack of hope, affected decisions you have made?

_____

_____

_____

_____

What needs to happen before you have more hope in your life?

_____

_____

_____

_____

Life Outlook

Which are you, an optimist or pessimist? Why do you believe this?

_____

_____

_____

_____

How long have you felt like an optimist or pessimist? What brought this on?

_____

_____

_____

_____

How does your environment affect the way you view the world?

_____

_____

_____

_____

Think of a time when you viewed a situation as negative, and yet, something positive came out of it?

_____

_____

_____

_____

_____

How can you begin to view the world in an even more positive light?

_____

_____

_____

_____

Optimistic Friends in My Life

It is advantageous to surround yourself with friends who are optimistic.

Complete the table below. Use name codes.

My Optimistic Friends	How They Show Their Optimism
(Ex: EAL)	*(When I am upset he always tries to show me the bright side of the situation.)*

© 2012 WHOLE PERSON ASSOCIATES, 210 WEST MICHIGAN ST., DULUTH MN 55802-1908 ▪ 800-247-6789

Pessimistic Friends in My Life

It is advantageous to reduce or eliminate contact with friends in your life who are pessimistic. Complete the table below. Use name codes.

My Pessimistic Friends	How They Show Their Pessimism
(Ex: LBC)	*(When I am upset he always finds more reasons for me to be upset about the situation.)*

Reconstructing My Attitude

When you find yourself getting stuck in a cycle of negative thinking, what is one method you can try to restructure your thinking from pessimistic to optimistic?

Consider the situation, as an example, of "I'm not good enough to pass math."

- When you feel yourself becoming negative, identify your negative thoughts: *"I'm not good enough," "I'm not smart enough," "She's better at it than me," "I'm terrible at math."*

- Think about the accuracy of your statements. What is the proof they are accurate? When you look at them objectively, what do you learn?

- Think of positive ways to restructure these thoughts. *"I know things I am good at," "I will do the best I can," "I can get help."*

- Take action: *"I will figure out what I can do alone," "I will ask if she will tutor me with the hard parts, and I will help her with her writing skills."*

Now You Try

State a time when you had negative thoughts about a situation that kept you from following through.

_____

_____

What were your negative thoughts?

_____

_____

How accurate were they? Was there proof?

_____

_____

How could you have restructured your thinking?

_____

_____

How could you have taken action?

_____

_____

Obstacles in My Life

It is important for you to identify and confront the obstacles in your life. These obstacles could be relationships, attitudes, habits, situations, things you lack such as more education or experience. In the table below, in the left hand column, describe obstacles and how they block you. In the right hand column, describe what you can do to overcome those obstacles. Use name codes.

A Life Obstacle and How It Blocks Me	What I Can Do to Overcome This Obstacle
(Ex: MLD and SBD are getting a divorce.)	*(I will support their choice and try not to be judgmental.)*

My School/Volunteer/Work Obstacles

It is also important for you to identify and confront the obstacles at school, volunteer job or work place. These obstacles could be people, attitudes, habits, situations, things you lack such as training. In the table that follows, describe the obstacles in your life in the left-hand column, and then in the right-hand column list some ways you might be able to overcome these obstacles. Use name codes.

School/Volunteer/Work Obstacles and How They Block Me	What I Can Do to Overcome This Obstacle
(Ex: I don't know which classes I want to take next year.)	*(I will talk with the counselor or my favorite teacher.)*

© 2012 WHOLE PERSON ASSOCIATES, 210 WEST MICHIGAN ST., DULUTH MN 55802-1908 • 800-247-6789

Overcoming Obstacles

Obstacles are present in the lives of everyone, but optimistic people continually work to find ways to overcome those obstacles.

From the completed *Obstacles in My Life* handout, page 25, what theme(s) do you see related to the obstacles in your life?

_____

_____

_____

_____

From the completed *My School/Volunteer/Work Obstacles* handout, page 26, what theme(s) do you see related to those obstacles?

_____

_____

_____

_____

What goals can you immediately begin working toward to help overcome your obstacles in all of these areas?

_____

_____

_____

_____

What positive risks can you take, even though you may be reluctant, to help you overcome these obstacles?

_____

_____

_____

_____

Building an Optimistic Outlook

Optimistic people look for the good qualities in other people. List the optimistic people whom you know and identify their good qualities. Use name codes.

People I Know	Positive Qualities
Ex: MSS	*She does not get overly upset when unexpected things happen in her life. She takes things in stride by looking for positive possibilities.*

Creating Goals

Optimistic people set small attainable goals and then reward themselves when the goals are attained.

Goals	Ways I Will Reward Myself When My Goal Is Achieved
Ex: To get better grades than I have been.	*I will talk to some people who get better grades to help me develop better study skills.*

Optimism Quotations

Choose two of these quotes. How does each speak to your feelings about optimism? If you disagree with a quote, write about it as well.

Optimism is essential to achievement and it is also the foundation of courage and true progress. ~ **Nicholas Butler**

Too much of a good thing is wonderful. ~ **May West**

My optimism for life carried through my work. ~ **John Dyer**

One of the things I learned the hard way was that it doesn't pay to get discouraged. Keeping busy and making optimism a way of life can restore your faith in yourself. ~ **Lucille Ball**

Optimism is the faith that leads to achievement. Nothing can be done without hope and confidence. ~ **Helen Keller**

The average pencil is seven inches long, with just a half-inch eraser – in case you thought optimism was dead. ~ **Robert Brault**

Most of the shadows of this life are caused by standing in one's own sunshine. ~ **Ralph Waldo Emerson**

_____

_____

_____

_____

_____

_____

_____

_____

_____

_____

_____

_____

_____

My Plan

Journal about how you plan on becoming a more optimistic person.

_____

_____

_____

_____

_____

_____

_____

_____

_____

_____

_____

_____

_____

_____

_____

_____

_____

_____

_____

_____

_____

_____

With whom can you share your plan? Who can support you? Use name codes.

_____

_____

_____

_____

_____

_____

Benefits of Optimism

With optimistic thinking, there is a greater chance of being able to . . .

- handle stress

- be my best at whatever I do

- reach my goals

- recover quickly from illness

- choose optimistic and supportive friends

- maintain a healthy emotional, mental and physical well-being

- believe in myself

- expect good things to happen to me

- be willing to take positive risks

- enjoy healthy relationships

Optimism . . .

- can be learned

- allows one to dip into inherent strengths

- helps overcome obstacles

- contributes to a better performance

- assists people in problem solving situations

- provides energy to achieve goals

- protects against depression, substance abuse, behavioral problems

- develops strengths to persist and persevere

- supports one when life presents challenges

- contributes to a better outlook

- encourages hope

- allows one to be aware of the needs of others

- builds confidence in the future

- develops a more positive attitude

Optimism is expecting the best possible outcome from any given situation.

SECTION II:

Sense of Control Scale

Name_____

Date_____

Sense of Control Scale Directions

Sense of control refers to your beliefs about what causes the good or bad things that happen in your life. It is the extent to which you believe that you can control the events that affect you, in the many aspects of your life.

This scale contains 30 statements related to three important resistance resources that can help build protection against stress. Read each of the statements and decide whether or not the statement describes you. If the statement describes you, circle the number under the YES column, next to that item. If the statement does not describe you, circle the number under the NO column, next to that item.

In the following example, the circled number under YES indicates the statement is descriptive of the person completing the inventory.

	YES	**NO**
Others control my life	(1)	2

This is not a test and there are no right or wrong answers. Do not spend too much time thinking about your answers. Your initial response will be the most true for you. Be sure to respond to every statement.

(Turn to the next page and begin)

Sense of Control Scale

	YES	NO
Others control my life	1	2
I create my own destiny	2	1
I determine the course of my life	2	1
When I make a plan, I make it work	2	1
I am often the victim of forces I cannot understand	1	2
I trust my life to fate	1	2
Heredity determines the success of people	1	2
I believe that what is going to happen will happen.	1	2
Teens cannot change basic behavior patterns	1	2
Teens can rise above their home-life upbringing	2	1

C - TOTAL = _____

	YES	NO
I rarely plan too far ahead.	1	2
I usually reach the goals I set for myself	2	1
Luck has nothing to do with being successful	2	1
To get ahead, I must be in the right place at the right time	1	2
If I work hard enough, I can succeed	2	1
Teens get ahead in life mainly because they know someone	1	2
I believe I can change tomorrow by what I do today	2	1
Teens can get their own way if they keep trying.	2	1
When good things happen it's often because of hard work.	2	1
With enough effort, people can get what they want	2	1

(Continued on the next page)

(Sense of Control Scale continued)

P - TOTAL = _____

	YES	NO
When I get what I want, it is because of my actions 2		1
Some people are just born lucky. 1		2
I believe that wishing can make good things happen. 1		2
A lucky charm works 1		2
Getting what I want has little to do with luck 2		1
I have a good luck charm that I rely on. 1		2
I believe it is better to be smart than lucky. 2		1
Some teens get all of the lucky breaks 1		2
I make my own luck 2		1
Bad luck seems to follow me around 1		2

L = TOTAL = _____

(Go to the Scoring Directions on the next page)

Sense of Control Scale Scoring Directions

Your sense of control can be either internal or external. An internal sense of control is one in which you are in control of your own life. An external sense of control is one in which you believe that your environment or other people control your life.

For the sections you just completed, add the numbers that you circled in each section. Transfer the totals below. For your overall Sense of Control total, add the three scores.

C — Control   **Total   = ** _____

**P — Persistence Total   = ** _____

L — Luck   **Total   = ** _____

**Sense of Control   Total   = ** _____

Profile Interpretation

INDIVIDUAL SCALE SCORE	TOTAL FOR ALL THREE SCALES SCORES	RESULT	INDICATIONS
Scores from 17 to 20	Scores from 51 to 60	High	High Scores indicate that you believe your behavior is guided by your own personal decisions and efforts.
Scores from 14 to 16	Scores from 40 to 50	Moderate	Moderate Scores indicate that you believe your behavior is guided by a combination of your own efforts and some external circumstances.
Scores from 10 to 13	Scores from 30 to 39	Low	Low Scores indicate that you believe your behavior is guided by fate, luck or other external circumstances.

Whether you scored Low, Moderate or High, the following exercises will help you build sense of control resources.

The Development of Sense of Control

Sense of control develops from a combination of family and cultural influences and previous experiences. Let's examine those factors in your life. Use name codes.

What does your mother/female caregiver believe about the factors that lead to success?

_____

_____

_____

What does your mother/female caregiver believe about luck leading to success?

_____

_____

_____

What did your father/male caregiver believe about the factors that lead to success?

_____

_____

_____

What did your father/male caregiver believe about luck leading to success?

_____

_____

_____

How do your cultural, spiritual and/or religious beliefs affect your thoughts about your destiny?

_____

_____

_____

If you don't know what your family believes about success, it might be interesting to ask them.

Contributing to My Successes

It is important to look at how you have contributed to the successes in your life.

The Success	How I Contributed to the Success
Ex: I will graduate with a high GPA.	*I studied hard, asked people for help when I needed it, and worked in the summer for spending money.*

My Disappointments

It is equally important to look at the disappointments in your life. In the table that follows, describe your disappointments and the ways you contributed to your future in a negative way.

The Disappointment	How I Contributed to My Future in a Negative Way
Ex: I dropped out of school	I did not go to class. I listened to my friends who said school was not important and it would be more fun to be with them. They were wrong.

How can you have more of a positive impact in future situations?

_____

_____

_____

Gaining More Control over My Daily Life

One way to have more control over what happens daily is to create a situation for yourself where good things can happen. You may need to change your patterns within your family, and social relationships, and school and work environment.

Better Situations for Me	How This Can Help
Ex: Turn OFF my cell phone and other electronic devices for two hours each night.	*I will be able to study without interruptions and get more done in a shorter amount of time.*

Action Plan

This section will help you develop an action plan to take more control of your life. With a plan, you can exert more control over your life than you ever imagined.

Step 1 — My Life

Identify areas in your life where you feel dissatisfied or in a rut. Think about where you feel unfulfilled — school, social and work relationships, family responsibilities, hopes and dreams, etc.

State one of your unfulfilled areas: (*Ex: doing well in school*)

_____

Step 2 — Look at Your Attitude

Take a look at your attitude as it relates to the area you indentified above in Step 1. It is through your attitude that you limit yourself and remain stuck. By confronting and changing your attitude, you can empower yourself to make positive changes in your life.

Think about the negative and limiting attitudes. What might be keeping you stuck?

OTHER'S BELIEFS ABOUT MY ABILITY TO INFLUENCE MY LIFE. Use name codes.

(*Ex: MFG told me "You don't have the brains you were born with."*)

_____

_____

_____

PERSONAL LIMITATIONS AND BELIEFS

What attitudes and beliefs do you have about yourself that limit your exerting control over your situation?

Example:
  - *I will never succeed*   - *I am not as smart as my siblings*

Now you try. List the personal limitation and beliefs you have about yourself:

_____

_____

_____

(Continued)

(Action Plan continued)

ATTITUDES ABOUT OTHERS

You may have negative attitudes about other people in your life.

Example:

- *DSJ thinks he is so smart*
- *MLQ doesn't respect what I have to say*
- *BLS doesn't think I deserve a promotion at my job*
- *EFH is to blame*

Now you try. List the negative attitudes and beliefs you have about people in your life. Use name codes.

_____

_____

_____

_____

_____

_____

_____

_____

Remember, it is what YOU believe about yourself, NOT what others believe about you, that can influence you in either a positive or a negative way.

Step 3 — Changing Your Attitude

In step 3, you have the opportunity to identify ways to change negative attitudes and move past the issues you identified in Step 1. These attitudes and beliefs can be overcome with a few simple techniques:

- Notice when negative thoughts pop into your head. Stop that negative self-talk, challenge it and substitute more positive self-talk.

- Now that you have identified negative thoughts and attitudes in Step 2, think about whether the thoughts are accurate, or not. What evidence is there for their accuracy?

- In the table on the next page list your negative thoughts and the evidence you have for their accuracy.

(Continued)

(Action Plan continued)

Negative Attitudes	Evidence for These Attitudes
Ex: I'm not smart enough to go to college.	*LZA told me.*

(Continued)

(Action Plan continued)

Repeat your negative thoughts from the previous page in the first column and then substitute positive thoughts for those negative thoughts.

Negative Attitudes	Substitute Positive Thoughts from the First Column
(Ex: I am not smart enough to go to college.)	*I am smart enough to go to college. I will start with a community college where I can receive personalized assistance.*

(Continued)

(Action Plan continued)

STEP 4 — Set Goals for Change

Goals can help you regain control in your life. List several of your goals and hopes related to the area in which you feel stuck. For example:

- *I want to get a job where I can help people*
- *I want to further my education*
- *I want to have more supportive friends*
- *I want to pass math*

List two goals related to the unfulfilled area you identified in Step 1:

Goal #1: _____

_____

Goal #2: _____

_____

Step 5 — Identify Short-term Steps — Begin Moving Toward Your Goals

These short-term steps are action-oriented activities to move you toward the general goals you identified in the last step. In the table the follows, list the short-term steps you will begin taking to reach ONE of your goals and the deadlines you set for completing each step.

Steps I Will Take for One of My Goals Ex: I want to pass math	Deadlines for Completing Steps
Ex: I will make an appointment with a counselor.	*tomorrow*
Ex: I will keep my appointment with the counselor, even if I am apprehensive!	*next week*
Ex: I will listen to all suggestions and act on one of the counselor's suggestions that seems most comfortable for me.	*the next day*

(Continued)

(Action Plan continued)

STEP 6 — Take Action *(to be completed after Step 5 is finished)*
It's time to take action by taking control of your life.

Steps I Have Completed

Steps I Am Having Trouble Completing

Why do you think you are having trouble completing some of the steps? Can you revise them to make them more doable?

_____

_____

_____

How has this process, or how will this process, help you to take greater control of the events in your life?

_____

_____

_____

To Know What I Can and Cannot Control

In life, there are certain things that you cannot control. It is important that you identify them and not waste time, emotional and physical energy, trying to change them. In the following boxes, list what you can and cannot control:

I Can Control . . .	I Cannot Control . . .
Ex: Getting to school on time every day.	*The time that school begins each day.*

Sense of Control Quotes

Choose three quotations and describe what each one means to you.

Could we change our attitude, we should not only see life differently, but life itself would come to be different. ~ **Katherine Mansfield**

_____

_____

The size of your success is measured by the strength of your desire; the size of your dream, and how you handle disappointment along the way. ~ **Robert Kiyosaki**

_____

_____

No life is so hard that you can't make it easier by the way you take it. ~ **Ellen Glasgow**

_____

_____

We must accept finite disappointment but never lose infinite hope. ~ **Martin Luther King, Jr.**

_____

_____

I long to accomplish a great and noble task, but it is my chief duty to accomplish small tasks as if they were great and noble. ~ **Helen Keller**

_____

_____

I cannot always control what goes on outside. But I can always control what goes on inside. ~ **Wayne Dyer**

_____

_____

Control your emotion or it will control you. ~ **Charles Popplestown**

_____

_____

Your Sense of Control

Why is it so important to understand your sense of control?

_____

_____

_____

_____

_____

_____

_____

_____

_____

_____

_____

_____

_____

_____

_____

What have you learned about your sense on control?

_____

_____

_____

_____

_____

_____

_____

_____

_____

_____

_____

_____

_____

_____

_____

To Change Your Sense of Control . . .

- Realize that you have choices that can change many situations.

- Know that you can always change your attitude to alter how you view a situation.

- Brainstorm various courses of action with people you trust.

- Take responsibility for your own success.

- Recognize what you can change.

- Know what you cannot change.

- Remember that you can learn to be more internally oriented.

- Change your negative "self-talk" to positive "self-talk."

Results of a Healthy Sense of Control

- Self-determination increases as you become more responsible for your actions

- Stress management skills develop

- Achievement orientation sharpens

- Decision making skills improve

- Problem solving skills expand

- Responsibility deepens for one's own limitations

- Self-confidence grows

- Recognition develops of one's personal responsibility for self-control, seeking opportunities, and investigating effects of others.

SECTION III:
Sense-of-Self Scale

Name_____

Date_____

Sense-of-Self Scale Directions

Resilient people have an excellent sense-of-self. They believe in themselves, understand themselves, and maintain confidence in their abilities. The purpose of this assessment is to help you become aware of your self-esteem, self-confidence and self-concept.

This scale contains 24 statements divided into three sections. Read each statement and decide how true the statement is for you. In the following example, the circled "2" indicates that the statement is Somewhat True for the person completing the inventory:

	True	Somewhat True	Not True
SECTION I			
I find it difficult to like myself	1	(2)	3

This is not a test and there are no right or wrong answers. Do not spend too much time thinking about your answers. Your initial response will be the most true for you. Be sure to respond to every statement.

(Turn to the next page and begin)

Sense-of-Self Scale

	True	Somewhat True	Not True
SECTION I			
I find it difficult to like myself	1	2	3
I believe I have nothing to contribute to the world	1	2	3
I measure success against my own standards, not those of my friends.	3	2	1
I worry about what my friends think about me.	1	2	3
I appreciate my own worth and importance	3	2	1
I see my peers as being better than me	1	2	3
I am as good as anyone else	3	2	1
I am able to overcome tough times and setbacks	3	2	1

I – TOTAL = _____

	True	Somewhat True	Not True
SECTION II			
I live my life based on what I truly value.	3	2	1
I take responsibility for my choices and actions	3	2	1
I don't like how I look	1	2	3
I am honest with myself	3	2	1
I have trouble accepting myself as I am now	1	2	3
On the whole, I am satisfied with myself	3	2	1
I do not handle change very well	1	2	3
I know I have potential, but I don't know what it is	1	2	3

II – TOTAL = _____

	True	Somewhat True	Not True
SECTION III			
I tend to do what is asked of me rather than what I feel is right.	1	2	3
I am willing to take positive risks to achieve what I want	3	2	1
I usually admit my mistakes and learn from them	3	2	1
It is difficult for me to accept compliments.	1	2	3
I handle new situations with comfort and ease.	3	2	1
If something looks too difficult, I avoid it	1	2	3
I believe that if I work hard, I will succeed	3	2	1
I often feel the need to be right	1	2	3

III – TOTAL = _____

(Go to the Scoring Directions on the next page)

Sense-of-Self Scale Scoring Directions

Add the totals for each section of the scale and then transfer those totals below.

SECTION I   Self-Esteem   TOTAL = _____

SECTION II   Self-Concept   TOTAL = _____

SECTION III   Self-Confidence   TOTAL = _____

To define your overall Sense-of-Self total, total the three scores above.

SENSE-OF-SELF TOTAL = _____

Profile Interpretation

INDIVIDUAL SCALE SCORE	TOTAL SCALES SCORES	RESULT	INDICATIONS
Scores from 8 to 13	Scores from 24 to 40	Low	You tend to have less sense-of-self than resilient people. However, you can develop a greater sense-of-self and become more resilient.
Scores from 14 to 18	Scores from 41 to 55	Moderate	You tend to have a pretty good sense-of-self, approaching that of resilient people. However, you can develop a greater sense-of-self and become more resilient.
Scores from 19 to 24	Scores from 56 to 72	High	You tend to have a good sense-of-self, similar to that of resilient people. However, you can continue to develop a greater sense-of-self and become even more resilient.

The higher your score on this scale, the greater your sense-of-self. In the areas in which you score in the Moderate or Low range, make an effort to continue to build your self-esteem, self-concept and self-confidence. No matter whether you scored Low, Moderate or High, the exercises and activities that follow will help you build your resiliency.

Sense-of-Self

Your sense-of-self is a unique combination of your self-esteem, self-concept and self-confidence. Each of these three factors is equally important, and all three are constantly interacting to help you to determine your sense-of-self.

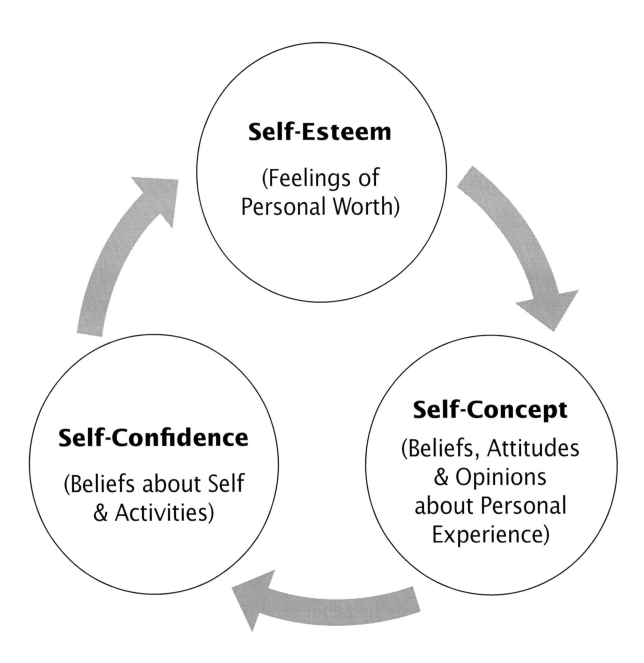

Self-Esteem

My Good Points

You can raise your self-esteem by recognizing your abilities, skills and personal qualities. In the spaces below, make a list of the characteristics you like about yourself.

My Good Points	Describe These Good Points
Abilities	*Ex: I am great at English and writing.*
Skills	*Ex: I am very organized.*
Personal Qualities	*Ex: I am extremely compassionate.*

(Continued on the next page)

(Self-Esteem continued)

What Others Like About Me

What Others Like About Me	Describe These Good Points
Abilities	*Ex: I am a great baseball left-fielder and help my team.*
Skills	*Ex: I remember trivia.*
Personal Qualities	*Ex: I am supportive.*

Summarize your qualities based on the previous two tables.

_____

_____

_____

_____

_____

_____

Self-Criticisms

Sometimes we have an inner voice that tells us how wrong, bad or undeserving we are. This inner critic can keep us from feeling good about ourselves. List the characteristics you do not like about yourself, ways you show your characteristics and how you can change them.

Characteristics I Do Not Like About Myself	How I Show These Characteristics	How I Can Change them
Ex: I am not assertive enough.	I do whatever someone tells me to do and ignore what I want to do.	I can say "no" in an honest, open and direct way, and do what I believe to be right.

Self-Concept

Your self-concept is how you view yourself. A healthy self-concept is important in developing resiliency since the way you view yourself determines how you experience life. If your self-concept is positive, you will experience life that way. However, if your self-concept is fragile, and you are insecure, you will tend to feel overwhelmed when facing challenges. Your self-concept can be described as who you are and how you fit into the world. The following exercises are designed to help you develop a healthy self-concept.

Know Yourself

How are you unique?

_____

_____

_____

_____

_____

What would you like to change about yourself?

_____

_____

_____

_____

_____

In what ways are you worthwhile?

_____

_____

_____

_____

_____

(Continued on the next page)

(Self-Concept continued)

What do you accept about yourself?

_____

_____

_____

_____

_____

About what do you criticize yourself? How accurate are these criticisms?

_____

_____

_____

_____

_____

What about your appearance do you like?

_____

_____

_____

_____

_____

What about your appearance do you dislike?

_____

_____

_____

_____

_____

Self-Confidence

We are not born with self-confidence; we learn and develop self-confidence from our interactions with family, friends and others. Self-confidence can be learned and unlearned. The following activities can help you develop greater self-confidence.

Role Models

Think about the people you know who appear to have self-confidence. In the left hand column of the table below, list three people who, by your observations and by their mannerisms, could be role-models of self-confidence. These people may be dead or alive, famous people from history, or people you know. In the middle column, list what you think might have helped them to be self-confident and in the third column describe how they act.

Role Models	What Made Them Confident	How They Acted
Ex: Helen Keller	Even though people told her she would be limited, she refused to believe that.	Instead of acting like a victim, she took responsibility for her life.

(Continued on the next page)

(Self-confidence continued)

Comparisons

One way you can develop greater self-confidence is by not comparing yourself negatively with other people. The first step in doing so is to identify those people with whom you typically compare yourself. In the table that follows, identify the people with whom you compare yourself, how you compare yourself and something positive about yourself. Use name codes.

Who I Compare Myself To	How I Compare Myself To Them	What I Have Going for Me!
Ex: BFS	*I compare my grades to his.*	*I am a good singer.*

(Continued on the next page)

(Self-Confidence continued)

My Successes

Remember your successes from the past. Success increases sense-of-self and self-esteem. In the table that follows, draw pictures or write about your greatest successes in the various aspects of your life. Feel free to use blank sheets of paper to continue with more successes.

Success With My Family	Success in School
Success at Work/Volunteering	Success in the Community
Success in my Spare Time	Other Successes

(Continued on the next page)

(Self-Confidence continued)

Taking Positive Risks

Positive risks are actions in which you "step out of the box," think creatively and do something you ordinarily would not do. These actions do not risk your health or well-being, and affect you in a positive way. *(Ex: XYZ has never sung in front of people, but decided to join the choir.)*

What personal risks have you taken in the past that have led to success for you?

_____

_____

_____

_____

What personal risks have you not taken in the past that probably would have led to greater self-confidence?

_____

_____

_____

_____

What school, job or volunteer risks have you taken in the past that have led to success for you?

_____

_____

_____

_____

What school, job or volunteer risks have you not taken in the past that probably would have led to greater self-confidence?

_____

_____

_____

_____

(Continued on the next page)

(Self-Confidence continued)

Taking Positive Risks

In the following table write about risks that you might take in the future that can lead to greater success, happiness and achievement.

A Positive Risk I Can Take	How It Can Lead to Success
Ex: Accept a volunteer position on the weekends at the local animal shelter.	*Ex: I'll feel good about myself by helping homeless animals. If I like it, I might consider a career as a veterinarian.*

Sense-of-Self Quotations

Place a check mark by the quote(s) that you feel might inspire you to have greater sense-of-self. You can cut the quotes out and post them by your computer, on the inside of your notebook or in your wallet. At the bottom of the page, write about why those quote(s) spoke to you.

No one can make you feel inferior without your consent. ~ **Eleanor Roosevelt**

Someone's opinion of you does not have to become your reality. ~ **Les Brown**

It took me a long time not to judge myself through someone else's eyes. ~ **Sally Field**

You were not born a winner, and you were not born a loser. You are what you make yourself to be. ~ **Lou Holtz**

Self-trust is the first secret of success. ~ **Ralph Waldo Emerson**

Aerodynamically the bumblebee shouldn't be able to fly, but the bumblebee doesn't know that so it goes on flying anyway. ~ **Mary Kay Ash**

You have within you right now, everything you need to deal with whatever the world can throw at you. ~ **Brian Tracy**

_____

_____

_____

_____

_____

_____

_____

_____

My Characteristics

What positive qualities did you learn that you possess?

_____

_____

_____

_____

_____

_____

In what ways will you continue to make the most of these qualities?

_____

_____

_____

_____

_____

What personal negative characteristics did you learn that you possess?

_____

_____

_____

_____

_____

How will you go about changing these characteristics?

_____

_____

_____

_____

_____

_____

Sense-of-Self and Resilience

How can a greater sense-of-self help you to be more resilient?

_____

_____

_____

_____

_____

_____

_____

_____

_____

_____

_____

_____

_____

_____

_____

_____

_____

_____

_____

_____

_____

_____

_____

_____

_____

_____

_____

_____

_____

_____

_____

The Sense-of-Self Circle

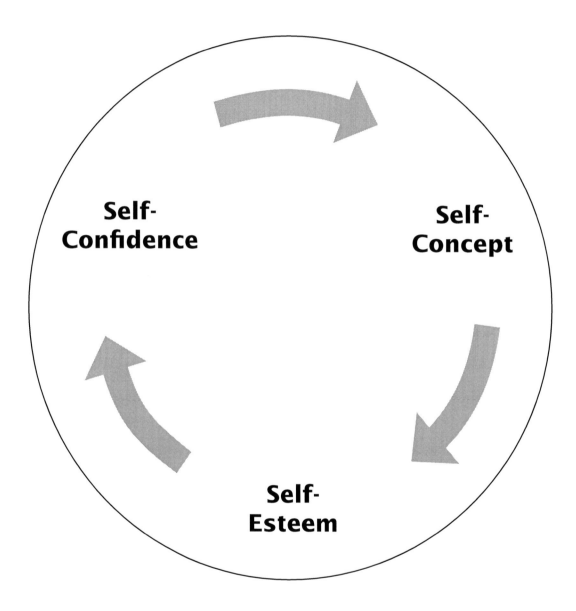

Facts about Sense-of-Self

- Perceived successes and failures impact one's sense-of-self.

- People see themselves differently from the ways others perceive them.

- Sense-of-self is relatively stable but can be learned and changed.

- People behave in ways consistent with their sense-of-self.

- Faulty thinking patterns can create a negative sense-of-self.

- Self-criticism can negatively affect one's sense-of-self.

- Sense-of-self consists of three parts:
  Self-concept
  Self-esteem
  Self-confidence

SECTION IV:
Ability to Bounce Back Scale

Name_____

Date_____

Ability to Bounce Back Scale Directions

People who are able to bounce back from a difficult situation or crisis, tend to feel that what happens in their lives is a result of their own actions and within their control. On the other hand, people who act and believe that they are victims, tend to feel life has not treated them fairly. They feel everyone and everything else is to blame for what happens in their lives. This scale helps to identify your current mind-set. Read each statement carefully and circle the number of the response that describes you best.

	TRUE	USUALLY	RARELY	NOT TRUE
1. I have trouble taking positive risks 1		2	(3)	4

In the above example, the circled 3 indicates that the responder sometimes has trouble taking positive risks.

This is not a test and there are no right or wrong answers. Do not spend too much time thinking about your answers. Your initial response will be the most true for you.
Be sure to respond to every statement.

(Turn to the next page and begin)

Ability to Bounce Back Scale

	TRUE	USUALLY	RARELY	NOT TRUE
1. I have trouble taking positive risks 1		2	3	4
2. I often ask why terrible things keep happening to me. 1		2	3	4
3. It does not bother me that I do not know the future 4		3	2	1
4. I tend to be judgmental of others 1		2	3	4
5. I use humor to help me through tough times 4		3	2	1
6. I find solutions to problems in times of trouble. 4		3	2	1
7. I accept differences in other people. 4		3	2	1
8. I do not perform well under pressure 1		2	3	4
9. I am able to bounce back when things get tough 4		3	2	1
10. I am not very flexible or adaptable 1		2	3	4
11. I want to leave the world better than I found it 4		3	2	1
12. I worry about what my friends say about me 1		2	3	4
13. I do not rely on my intuition very much. 1		2	3	4
14. I can be playful and childlike when it is appropriate 4		3	2	1
15. I am not very spontaneous 1		2	3	4
16. I enjoy learning things about myself 4		3	2	1
17. I care about the well-being of others 4		3	2	1
18. I have a hard time motivating myself. 1		2	3	4
19. I believe awful things are always going to happen to me 1		2	3	4
20. I am calm and focused under pressure 4		3	2	1
21. I am able to make light of myself even in difficult situations. . . 4		3	2	1
22. I dwell on mistakes I have made in the past 1		2	3	4
23. I keep going even if I am not sure of the outcome 4		3	2	1
24. I have a lot of regrets that I brood over 1		2	3	4
25. I tackle my problems and find solutions 4		3	2	1
26. I do not give up on tasks until they are completed 4		3	2	1
27. I sometimes feel like I am a victim. 1		2	3	4
28. I learn from my mistakes. 4		3	2	1
29. I view stressful situations as personal challenges 4		3	2	1
30. I worry about looking foolish. 1		2	3	4

TOTAL = _____

(Go to the Scoring Directions on the next page)

Ability to Bounce Back Scale
Scoring Directions

The scale you just completed is designed to help you explore whether your mind-set tends to allow you to bounce back from difficult situations or tends to promote your mind-set of being a victim. For each of the items on the previous page, total the scores you circled. Add your circled numbers and put that total on the line marked TOTAL at the end of the section and then transfer that number below.

Total _____ **Ability to Bounce Back**

Profile Interpretation

TOTAL SCALE SCORE	RESULT	INDICATIONS
Scores from 91 to 120	High	You tend to have a bounce-back mentality. You have control over what happens in your life and believe that good things are going to happen to you.
Scores from 60 to 90	Moderate	You tend to have a mix of the bounce-back and victim mentality.
Scores from 30 to 59	Low	You tend to have more of a victim mentality and it seems that you do not believe that you have control over what happens in your life or that good things are going to happen to you.

The exercises on the next pages will help you to further develop a bounce-back mentality.

Overcoming a Victim Mentality

A victim mentality is a self-defeating attitude with self-limiting thoughts about yourself that restrict you from reaching your full potential. It is a feeling that you cannot make changes in your life, and that you are living the life of a victim. Following are some activities and exercises to help you develop a bounce-back mentality.

People who have developed a victim mentality have often had many unfortunate circumstances in their past, leading to a negative, fatalistic attitude. What unfortunate circumstances have you experienced in the past? Identify these circumstances and how they affected you emotionally. Use name codes.

Negative Things That Occurred	How They Affected Me
Ex: MOJ lost his job of 15 years and was without one for quite a while.	*I was constantly worrying about our not having enough food to eat or getting new clothes. I was probably disagreeable to my friends and family.*

Overcoming Negative Messages

To overcome feeling like a victim, you need to release yourself from those negative messages you receive now or received in the past, that tell you to behave or think in a certain way. Think about the people in your life giving you negative messages about how to think, act or feel. List those people in your life (teachers, parents, friends, siblings, relatives, religious leaders, etc.) and the things they tell you. Then, in the last column, reverse the negative message to make it more positive. Use name codes.

People From My Life	Things They Say	How Have You, or Can You, Reverse This Message?
Ex: LHF	You're boring. You never want to do anything fun.	My ideas and LHF's ideas about fun are different. I don't need to like the same activity she does.

Invest in Yourself

By investing in yourself, you can make yourself more valuable in a variety of roles. Think about ways that you can feel empowered in situations you might encounter. List the ways that you can make yourself more valuable. Use name codes.

Situations	How I Can Invest in Myself
Ex: Friends	*I can stick to my values regardless of the pressure I get from my friends.*
Friends	
Education	
Community	
Health & Wellness	
Family	
Other	

Take More Responsibility

People with a bounce-back mentality take responsibility for what happens in their lives. Instead of blaming others for the bad things that happen, they are empowered by taking total responsibility for what happens to them. List the ways you can take more responsibility for your life. Use name codes.

Situations	How I Can Take More Responsibility
Ex: Friends	*I will be more assertive in an open, honest and direct way, when my friends are pressuring me to do things I don't want to do.*
Friends	
Education	
Community	
Health & Wellness	
Family	
Other	

Learn From Your Experiences

People with a bounce-back mentality are able to look at their experiences and find ways to use them to be more effective. List some of the negative things that have happened to you and what you can learn from these situations. Use name codes.

Negative Things in My Life	What I Can Learn
Ex: I failed a class.	*I need to keep up with my homework every day and ask for help if I need it.*

Excuses

People with a bounce-back mentality do not blame or use excuses to explain their behavior or the behavior of others. Use name codes.

What kind of things have you blamed on your circumstances?

(Ex: My inability to do well in school.)

_____

_____

_____

_____

_____

What excuses do you use?

(Ex: BMS does not have time to help me.)

_____

_____

_____

_____

How do excuses keep you from taking healthy risks?

(Ex: I'm not smart enough to go to college, so why try to get good grades?)

_____

_____

_____

_____

How do excuses keep you from taking responsibility?

(Ex: Since BMS does not have time to help me, it's her fault.)

_____

_____

_____

_____

Staying in the Present vs. Dwelling on the Past

People with a bounce-back mentality do not dwell on the past or let the past influence their choices in the present or their vision for the future. Describe some influences from your past and how they may prevent you from being more successful in the future. Use name codes.

Influences from the Past	How This Might Prevent Me from Being Successful
Ex: MDH passed away when I was seven years old and I am growing up in a single-parent home.	*ELM is doing a great job in raising me, but I missed out on a father-figure in my life. I feel like I did not have the same good experiences as some of my friends.*

Prepare for the Future

People with a bounce-back mentality live in the present, but are aware of ways they can influence their future. Describe what you can do in the future to influence your life in a positive way and how it will empower you.

Ways I Will Influence My Future	How It Will Empower Me
Ex: I will ask JHZ to tutor me in science to raise my grade point average.	I will be able to apply and get accepted into a community college and then transfer to a university.

(Continued on the next page)

(Prepare for the Future continued)

What about the future is worrisome?

_____

_____

_____

_____

What can you continue to do to make your life better?

_____

_____

_____

_____

How can you let go of negative things that have happened to you?

_____

_____

_____

_____

What fears do you have about taking healthy risks?

_____

_____

_____

_____

What situations could you change by exerting a little more effort?

_____

_____

_____

_____

Get What You Feel You Deserve

People with a bounce-back mentality are not afraid to seek out and get what they feel they deserve. What are the things in your life that you feel you deserve?

Situations	Things I Feel I Deserve
Ex: Friends	*I feel I deserve friends who will support me and not try to coerce me to do things I don't want to do.*
Friends	
Education	
Work	
Health & Wellness	
Family	
Other	

Focus and Commitment

People with a bounce-back mentality often are able to focus on one thing in their life that gives them hope and meaning, even when life seems very challenging.

What is one important thing (person, project, faith, etc.) to which you are committed?

_____

_____

_____

_____

How do you focus your attention on it?

_____

_____

_____

_____

What is the result of your focused attention (hope for the future, sense of purpose, etc.)

_____

_____

_____

_____

How will you maintain your focus and commitment to it?

_____

_____

_____

_____

Bounce-Back Quotations

Read and think about the following quotes. Pick your favorite and describe how it applies to your past life, your current life, and how you want to live in the future. Write in the spaces provided below the quotes.

Above all, be the heroine of your life, not the victim. ~ **Nora Ephron**

No matter how far life pushes you down, no matter how much you hurt, you can always bounce back. ~ **Sheryl Swoopes**

When you realize the value of all life, you dwell less on what is past and concentrate more on the preservation of the future. ~ **Dian Fossey**

You build on failure. You use it as a stepping stone. Close the door on the past. You don't try to forget the mistakes, but you don't dwell on it. You don't let it have any of your energy, or any of your time, or any of your space. ~ **Johnny Cash**

Past _____

_____

_____

_____

_____

Current _____

_____

_____

_____

_____

Future _____

_____

_____

_____

_____

I Learned . . .

What will you do now to develop more of a bounce-back mentality?

_____

_____

_____

_____

_____

_____

_____

_____

_____

_____

_____

_____

From the activities in this chapter, what did you learn most about yourself?

_____

_____

_____

_____

_____

_____

_____

_____

_____

_____

_____

_____

_____

Handling it Differently

What are some situations that you wish you had handled differently?

_____

_____

_____

_____

_____

_____

_____

_____

_____

_____

_____

_____

_____

In retrospect, how would you handle those situations now?

_____

_____

_____

_____

_____

_____

_____

_____

_____

_____

_____

_____

Ways to Develop a Bounce-Back Mentality

Here's what I can do . . .

- Find new, more positive friends.

- Prepare for the future.

- Laugh and find humor in my day.

- Do not label myself or allow myself to be labeled

- Remind myself frequently of my positive qualities.

- Stay in the present without dwelling on the past.

- Overcome negative messages.

- Invest in myself.

- Take more responsibility for my own actions.

- Learn from my experiences.

- Be sure that the negative influences of the past do not negatively affect my future.

- Refrain from making excuses or blaming.

- Be certain that I am, or can become, the person I want to be.

Reasons People Maintain a Victim Mentality

Awareness of the benefits people derive from being a victim can help you to decide that you do not wish to be a victim, and that you will choose to take a healthier path.

Victims

- Victims get attention (sometimes pity) from others who want to help them.

- Victims don't take positive risks; they only take unhealthy risks.

- Victims don't take responsibility for their life; they blame others.

- Victims enjoy the self-pity and negative life.

- Victims often have a false sense of love and acceptance.

- Victims feel entitled to sympathy and kindness, even if it's not sincere.

- Victims don't take responsiblity for the decisions they make; they blame others.

- Victims like being treated more kindly because of their suffering, even if they are not respected.

SECTION V:
Types of Change Scale

Name_____

Date_____

Types of Change Scale

We all experience changes in our lives, yet we all feel and react in a different ways with varying degrees of success. Resilient teens are able to look at change as an opportunity. They control their negative emotions about change and influence the outcome of the change.

Whether changes you are going through or have experienced are physical, social, emotional, psychological or familial, you can use this scale to help you examine how effectively you deal with these changes when they occur.

The *Types of Change Scale*, divided into four sections, contains descriptors of the types of change you may be experiencing. Think about the changes you are currently experiencing in your life, those you have experienced recently, and those that you anticipate in the future. Place a check in the boxes that describe changes you are currently experiencing or have recently experienced. Then, place an X after those that you anticipate in the near future.

The following example shows that the person completing the assessment has dropped out of school and had a change in work supervisors, while in the future a change in job responsibilities is expected as well as another new supervisor.

The types of change:

> **I have experienced or am experiencing . . .** ☑
>
> **and those anticipated in the future** 🄷

School & Career Changes

❏ New or different school	❏	
☑ Dropping out of school	❏	
☑ Work or volunteer supervisor	🄷	
❏ New responsibilities	🄷	

This is not a test and there are no right or wrong answers. Do not spend too much time thinking about your answers. Your initial response will be the most true for you. Be sure to respond to every statement.

(Turn to the next page and begin)

Types of Change Scale

The types of change:

I have experienced or am experiencing . . . ☑
and those anticipated in the future . . . . . . ☒

School & Career Changes

I HAVE EXPERIENCED OR AM EXPERIENCING ☑	ANTICIPATED ☒
❑ New or different school	❑
❑ Dropping out of school	❑
❑ Work or volunteer supervisor	❑
❑ New responsibilities	❑
❑ Future decisions	❑
❑ New technology	❑
❑ Fitting in with peers	❑
❑ Making new friends	❑
❑ High academic expectations	❑
❑ Achieving good grades	❑
❑ Getting into a college	❑
❑ Thinking about career decisions	❑
❑ Search for a job	❑
❑ Recent dislike of school	❑
❑ Problems with a teacher(s)	❑
❑ Other	❑
❑ Other	❑
❑ Other	❑

Personal & Health Changes

I HAVE EXPERIENCED OR AM EXPERIENCING ☑	ANTICIPATED ☒
❑ Illness	❑
❑ Injury	❑
❑ Disability	❑
❑ Physical appearance	❑
❑ Suicidal thoughts	❑
❑ Religious beliefs	❑
❑ Social activities	❑
❑ Accident	❑
❑ Health	❑
❑ Illegal substances	❑
❑ Experiencing failure	❑
❑ Alcohol, inhalants or smoking	❑
❑ Legal problems	❑
❑ Depression	❑
❑ Alternative lifestyle	❑
❑ Other	❑
❑ Other	❑
❑ Other	❑

☑ S & C TOTAL = _____

☒ S & C TOTAL = _____

☑ P & H TOTAL = _____

☒ P & H TOTAL = _____

(Continued on the next page)

Types of Change Scale *(Continued)*

The types of change:

> **I have experienced or am experiencing . . . ☑**
> **and those anticipated in the future . . . . . . ☒**

Home & Caregiver Changes		
I HAVE EXPERIENCED OR AM EXPERIENCING ☑		**ANTICIPATED ☒**
❑ Residence		❑
❑ Marriage		❑
❑ Divorce		❑
❑ Separation		❑
❑ New siblings		❑
❑ Death of friend		❑
❑ Death of family member		❑
❑ Birth of a child		❑
❑ Remarriage		❑
❑ Blended family		❑
❑ Sibling rivalry		❑
❑ Health of household member		❑
❑ Care of older family member		❑
❑ Pregnancy		❑
❑ Foster care		❑
❑ Other		❑
❑ Other		❑
❑ Other		❑

Safety & Security Changes		
I HAVE EXPERIENCED OR AM EXPERIENCING ☑		**ANTICIPATED ☒**
❑ Peer Pressure		❑
❑ Pressure to use alcohol/drugs		❑
❑ Suicidal thoughts		❑
❑ Cyber bullying		❑
❑ Physical abuse		❑
❑ Sexual abuse		❑
❑ Unsafe sexual activity		❑
❑ Meeting new people online		❑
❑ Dating violence		❑
❑ Bullying by anyone		❑
❑ Driving		❑
❑ Using anabolic steroids		❑
❑ Carrying a weapon		❑
❑ Unsafe neighborhood		❑
❑ X-rated Internet sites		❑
❑ Other		❑
❑ Other		❑
❑ Other		❑

☑ **H & C TOTAL** = _____

☒ **H & C TOTAL** = _____

☑ **S & S TOTAL** = _____

☒ **S & S TOTAL** = _____

(Go to the Scoring Directions on the next page)

Types of Change Scale
Scoring Directions

Because it is a normal aspect of everyone's life, everyone experiences change. It is important to identify the aspects of your life in which you are experiencing major changes, become aware of them and notice how these changes affects you. This assessment will help you explore the various ways you are experiencing change in your life. For each of the sections, count the number of boxes in which you placed a ✔ and an **X**. Put that total on the line marked **TOTAL** at the end of each section.

Transfer your totals to the spaces below:

☑ _____ = **S & C (School & Career)**   TOTAL = _____ ☒

☑ _____ = **P & H (Personal & Health)**   TOTAL = _____ ☒

☑ _____ = **H & C (Home & Caregiver)**   TOTAL = _____ ☒

☑ _____ = **S & S (Safety & Security)**   TOTAL = _____ ☒

Profile Interpretation

Score Results	Indications
High	If you have a lot of ✔-marks, you are **currently experiencing a great deal of change** in that area. If you have a lot of **X**-marks, you are **anticipating** a great deal of change in that area, in the future.
Medium	If you have a medium amount of ✔-marks, you are **experiencing some change** in that area. If you have a medium amount of **X**-marks, you are **anticipating** some change in that area, in the future.
Low	If you have a low amount of ✔-marks, you are **not currently experiencing much change** in that area. If you have a low amount of **X**-marks, you **do not anticipate** much change in that area in the future.

No matter how you scored, low, medium or high, you will benefit from the exercises that follow.

Types of Change
Scale Descriptions

Read the descriptions below and complete the exercises included in this chapter. Whether you scored, low, medium or high, you will benefit from these exercises.

School & Career

People scoring high on the *School & Career Scale* are experiencing a great deal of change at school and in their work and volunteer activities. They may be changing schools or furthering their education, or they may be experiencing change at work in the form of new job responsibilities or new supervisors.

Personal & Health

People scoring high on the *Personal & Health Scale* are experiencing a great deal of change in their personal life and their physical and mental health. They may be experiencing an illness or be involved in an accident. They may be experiencing changes due to legal problems, changes in lifestyle, or changes in spiritual and/or religious beliefs.

Home & Caregiver

People scoring high on the *Home & Caregiver Scale* are experiencing a great deal of change in their home and life. They may be experiencing changes in their family life, caregiver and/or residence, and experiencing sibling rivalries, divorce, separation, and loss of loved ones and friends.

Safety & Security

People scoring high on the *Safety & Security Scale* are experiencing a great deal of change in their sense of safety and security. They may be experiencing physical or verbal abuse, bullying at home or school, cyber-bullying, pressure to drink alcohol or use drugs, and/or exposure to Internet violence.

Exploring Change
Use name codes.

What are some of the biggest changes that you have seen in your family and how have these changes affected you?

_____

_____

_____

_____

What are some of the biggest changes that you have seen at work or a volunteer position and how have these changes affected you?

_____

_____

_____

_____

What are some of the biggest changes that you have seen in your community and the larger society and how have these changes affected you?

_____

_____

_____

_____

What are some of the biggest changes that you have noticed in your friends and how have these changes affected you?

_____

_____

_____

_____

When Change Occurs

A change can affect every aspect of your life.
Identify a change that is happening or has happened in your life.

_____

Think about how you reacted to the change. How did you feel?

_____

_____

How did that change affect what you think about yourself?

_____

_____

What was your initial reaction?

_____

_____

How did it affect your thinking? (difficulty concentrating, forgetfulness, etc.)

_____

_____

How did it affect your interactions with people?

_____

_____

How did it affect your stress-level?

_____

_____

Changes in Your Life

Identify a change that is happening in your life and respond to the questions that follow.

_____

Opportunities

The way you view the change can be important in how well you are able to manage it.

How can you best cope with this change?

_____

_____

_____

How can you view the situation in a positive way?

_____

_____

_____

What can you learn from this situation?

_____

_____

_____

What new opportunities does the situation present?

_____

_____

_____

What types of positive risks will the change require you to take?

_____

_____

_____

My Strengths and Skills/Abilities

Identify your personal strengths, skills and abilities that you can rely on during a time of change.

Strengths	Skills / Abilities
(Ex: I am persistent, I am outgoing, etc.)	*(I am good at math, computers, etc.)*

Feelings

It is important to manage your feelings effectively during a time of change. Identify a change that has happened in your life.

_____

How did the change feel when it happened?

_____

_____

_____

_____

_____

_____

How do you feel now?

_____

_____

_____

_____

_____

_____

In the future, how can you control your emotional responses to manage the change?

_____

_____

_____

_____

_____

Acknowledging Feelings

It is helpful to acknowledge your feelings as you continue to face changes in your life. You may experience a variety of feelings that you need to explore and express. The following guide may help you. Use name codes.

Identify a change that is happening or has happened in your life.

_____

Denial – What denial feelings have you experienced because of this change?
("Is this really happening to me?")

_____

_____

_____

Bargaining – What bargaining feelings have you experienced because of this change?
("If I could do it again . . .")

_____

_____

_____

Anger – What angry feelings have you experienced because of this change?
("I hate JLP for doing this!")

_____

_____

_____

Sadness / Depression – What sad feelings have you experiencing because of this change?
("I give up.")

_____

_____

_____

Regaining Control

It helps to become more aware of what you can control and what you cannot control, as you work through the change that you are experiencing. Think about how you can gain greater control in these same situations.

Identify a change that is happening or has happened in your life.

_____

List the things that you can control and cannot control about this situation.

Things I Cannot Control	Things I Can Control
(Ex: I cannot control that my family needs to relocate.)	*(I can decide to move forward and make new friends.)*

Support

It might be helpful for you to talk with other people who have been in a similar situation to yours, or to a trusted adult (parent, counselor, teacher.) Use name codes.

Identify a change that is happening or has happened in your life.

_____

Identify some other people who are, or could be, a support system for you.

_____

_____

_____

_____

Based on the change in your life, what opportunities might now present themselves to you?

_____

_____

_____

_____

How can you be ready to be open to those opportunities?

_____

_____

_____

_____

Are there any silver linings or positives that you can imagine could come from the change?

_____

_____

_____

_____

_____

Influence

Any type of change, positive or negative, can dramatically influence life. Identify a change that is happening or has happened in your life.

_____

Think about this change and how it will probably influence your life.

Describe three different aspects (positive or negative) in your life.

1. _____

2. _____

3. _____

How will your life be the same?

1. _____

2. _____

3. _____

How will your life be different?

1. _____

2. _____

3. _____

What, if any, positive changes might happen?

1. _____

2. _____

3. _____

What, if any, negative changes might happen?

1. _____

2. _____

3. _____

© 2012 WHOLE PERSON ASSOCIATES, 210 WEST MICHIGAN ST., DULUTH MN 55802-1908 ▪ 800-247-6789

Quotations about Change

Our only security is our ability to change. ~ **John Lilly**

Change always comes bearing gifts. ~ **Price Pritchett**

If you don't like something change it: if you can't change it, change the way you think about it.
~ **Mary Engelbreit**

Change is the law of life. And those who look only to the past or present are certain to miss the future. ~ **John F. Kennedy**

Mighty oaks from little acorns grow. ~ **English proverb**

Growing up is never easy. You hold on to things that were. You wonder what's to come.
~ **The Wonder Years television show**

Check your favorite and write about it.

_____

_____

_____

_____

_____

_____

_____

_____

_____

_____

_____

_____

Managing Change Effectively

How can change provide you with opportunities?

_____
_____
_____
_____
_____
_____
_____
_____
_____
_____
_____
_____

What can you do to manage your feelings during a change?

_____
_____
_____
_____
_____
_____
_____
_____
_____
_____
_____
_____
_____

(Continued on the next page)

(Managing Change Effectively continued)

How can you gain control of your life during times of change?

_____

_____

_____

_____

_____

_____

_____

_____

_____

_____

_____

_____

_____

_____

How can you influence change when it does occur?

_____

_____

_____

_____

_____

_____

_____

_____

_____

_____

_____

_____

_____

_____

Change can be . . .

- interesting

- a chance to learn something new

- a way to empower you

- the key to put you in charge of your life

- the discovery of hidden opportunities

- motivation to get you unstuck, moving in the right direction

- the way to push you closer to your goals

- positive

Managing Stress During a Change

- Maintain a healthy diet

- Get enough sleep

- Walk or exercise daily

- Schedule fun things to do

- Find reasons to laugh

- Manage your time well

- Limit use of substances, caffeine, unhealthy foods and drinks

- Meditate or find quiet time daily

- Talk with supportive friends, family, a trusted adult

Whole Person Associates is the leading publisher
of training resources for professionals who empower
people to create and maintain healthy lifestyles.
Our creative resources will help you work effectively with
your clients in the areas of stress management,
wellness promotion, mental health and life skills.

Please visit us at our web site: **www.wholeperson.com**.
You can check out our entire line of products,
place an order, request our print catalog, and
sign up for our monthly special notifications.

Whole Person Associates
210 W Michigan
Duluth MN 55802
800-247-6789